PLAYFUL
HOMe

PLAYFUL HOMe

CREATIVE STYLE IDEAS FOR LIVING WITH KIDS

ANDREW WEAVING

RIZZOLI
NEW YORK

New York · Paris · London · Milan

CONTENTS

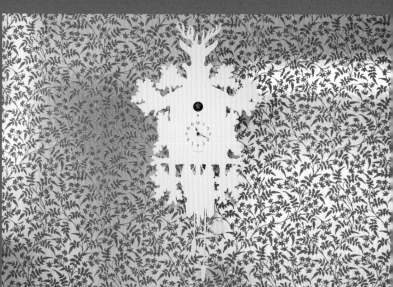

Left: My sister and I at a family Christmas, playing dominoes, one of our favorite games.
Right: A selection of kids' rooms from the 1950s and 1960s. All are very organized and grown up, with lots of storage and workspace. A child would dare not get anything out of place!

Introduction

Once upon a time there were homes where children were seen and not heard, and I am sure before that there where homes were they were neither seen nor heard. Often kept in rooms away from the parents, they were looked after by nannies and were generally not really part of the family. This, of course, was one extreme, and at the other extreme were children and parents together as one, perhaps living in one room, all pitching in, with the children growing up too soon and sent out to work early to help support the family. What a life children had, either over-privileged or under-nourished, not only in food, but with everything.

When I was a child in the late 1950s, I shared a bedroom with my sister, four years older than me. Since she was older, I remember our room was more decked out to suit her: we had pink tufted headboards that I recall helping my father make. He was very creative around the house and was always making or refurbishing things. I think the edging was gray, just to give a little masculinity to the room. I do not remember having much on display: no pictures on the walls or toys on my bed. We had lots of games,

but these were kept in cupboards and I only remember playing them on special occasions or at Christmas when all the family was together.

Both my parents had odd childhoods. My father's mother died when he was only six and his family was looked after by his elder sister; there was no time for fun and the home was not playful at all. They were hard times, the family was split up, and as soon as my father was old enough, he was on his way to war. My mother, on the other hand, was evacuated to South Africa at the outbreak of World War II. It was an adventure, but being in an entirely new place, and far away from her parents, was not much fun.

I suppose my parents' upbringings influenced how my sister and I were brought up. Our parents were not into material things and they spent more time with us having plain, simple fun. I remember being carried around the house on my father's toes, flying kites, doing lots of cutting out and making stuff, and, on the weekends, going fishing or to the seaside. I loved making little colored glasses out of multicolored candy wrappers. Playing a board

game, such as Monopoly, was a special treat. I do not remember having many manufactured toys until I was much older. Some of my friends at school had toy cars, castles, and soldiers, but I wasn't really interested in new things. On Sundays, my father would sometimes take me to street markets where there were lots of second-hand items. Most of my favorite stuff came from there!

Then we moved into a new house and it was a whole different thing; we had more space, white walls, shiny new floors and lots of light. I had space for a race track, I could choose my own wallpaper, and I could paint my bedroom chair bright orange. I had my own room at last! I helped decorate my room several times, and the walls were soon decked out with my favorite images. In my late teens, it eventually ended up to be a shrine to Biba, the iconic London fashion store, all dark brown, with big pillows, mirrors, and plaster ladies holding up the lamps. It was a place I could wrap myself up in and escape.

Many years later, I've become a parent by adopting a seven-year-old boy. Looking back at my childhood has made me think seriously about how to create a room that is playful, stimulating, and child friendly. I knew my son's favorite color was orange, and that he had many toys. He loved playing Legos and was creative. These few elements helped in creating a room that he loves; when he moved in he told me he felt like he had grown up in it.

Children's rooms are so much more important in today's interiors than they used to be, and more of us are creating "playful homes," where children can be at ease in any room in the house. As we are often bombarded with what's new for kids–computer games, applications for phones, video games, and other activities that keep children in their rooms–we sometimes forget that what children really need is interaction with others, environments that are playful and stimulating, and homes where they are actively included in the household, and where they are safe to play, whether inside or out.

This book features homes designed with children in mind. These spaces are diverse, but all were created to inspire fun and creativity.

BOYS' ROOMS

The boys have taken over the hallway of the house to have more space to play in. Its height and length make it the ideal space for high bounces on the trampoline and fast glides on the scooter.

13

There is no way you cannot notice that boys live here. Bikes, balls, and sneakers line the wall. The colorful screen prints lend sophistication and keep the space extra playful.

Boys will be boys! But we don't mean boys in the traditional cookie-cutter sense. Boys today can be whomever they want to be, inspired by whatever they choose, and, in particular, free to decorate their rooms however they see fit.

We used to think that a boy's room needed to be blue, or at least have blue in it, with perhaps a complementary color, such as red or yellow. But now, over the past decade especially, décor options have livened up and our ideas about what a boy's bedroom should look like have changed considerably.

Whether his room is inspired by superheroes or comic-strip characters, by sports, or perhaps travels overseas, as long as he loves his room and wants to spend time in it, anything goes. For that is the most important thing: kids need to have a say in their rooms' décor and ideally should be proud of their own spaces within the family home.

It can be easier to tackle a room's décor if you begin with a theme, which can then be developed. A signed football shirt, a skateboard, a home-made rocket, or an electric guitar handed down through the family can serve as inspiration, and even something as simple as favorite posters or maps or a favorite color can be enough to start with. From this initial concept you can then come up with a theme for the rest of the décor and furniture selection.

Of course, any child's room needs a few basic elements to work successfully: ample storage, display areas, work space, a comfy bed, enough room for sleepovers, good lighting, and the right kind of window treatment, depending on how the child likes to sleep.

When you look through the boys' rooms in these pages, you will find a vast array of styles, color schemes, arrangements, and themes. Each room is unique and each one reflects the boy's personality, proving that there are no rules to decorating boys' rooms except to be sure that the boy is part of the decorating too.

Three boys share this room. Their mom wanted them to have a room they all loved and the consensus was to use the color orange and airplanes.

Maps and globes are a fascination for many children. It's fun to map your vacation routes and pinpoint exactly where friends and family live.

Two boys share this BRIGHT AND SPACIOUS space with a loft bed and well-planned storage below. The table easily transforms into a FOOSBALL GAME when the mood takes them. The grass green carpet and TREE-LIKE WALLPAPER bring the outside in.

Bunks for four children encourage frequent sleepovers. Plenty of built-in storage keeps the floor area clear for hours of playtime. The windows behind are full height, bringing an open feel to the sleeping quarters.

Left: Ace's room is taken over by the full-size drum kit. But he seems to be enjoying it. The skateboard selection on the wall is a great decoration idea.

Right: Simple shelves are filled with vintage toys. The old tin buckets are perhaps too precious to use on the beach. The patchwork quilt on the bed is vintage, too.

This boy's room is a mix of bold colors, dark wood floors, and vintage furniture pieces. The walls and ceiling are hung with maps and planets. This is a room for a small boy to grow into, to add his favorite things as they are found and discovered.

These BUNKS resemble those on a SLEEPER TRAIN. What fun! Sheets of plywood with cutouts DISGUISE simple beds. The gingham curtains can be drawn when the kids want to get some SLEEP.

This futuristic pod bed has storage and a TV included. What more could a boy want? The custom-made ceiling light adds to the spacey feel.

In the playroom, a remote-control crane delivers Lego cars from one level to another. The Jonathan Adler pillows add a bit of graphic direction to the room.

Left: The storage unit on wheels has become a movable doll's house. On the wall, a low-hung, child-height hat rack is full of Ethan's favorite caps.

Right: The toy-car bed brings exciting dreams full of adventure in this boy's room. The Eames rocker brings some vintage charm.

Vintage Formica
tabletops make an
inspiring headboard
in this room. Above
is a stage for a
simple puppet show.

A large, round child-height table encourages simple playtime for all. Playing dominoes is one of our son's favorite games. The cat came from the local flea market.

This pod on legs is like sleeping in a spacecraft. A little ladder leads into the cozy and snug sleeping zone. The spindly legs keep the floor clear for many favorite toys.

GIRLS'
ROOMs

In an all-white room, the bunting, striped carpet, and fun chairs bring in a great dose of color. The child-size table and chairs are the hub of the room, ideal for tea parties.

This small room is cozy and inviting. The porthole window acts as a peephole to the garden below, and the bed is kept simple with plenty of striped pillows and flowery bedcovers.

If it's not pink, I do not want it! That's what I am sure many young girls have said about their bedrooms. But pink isn't everything. Where does this notion that pink is for girls but not for boys come from? It's true there are many girls' rooms that are not all pink, but on the other hand, I have been quite surprised to find pink creations in homes where you would least expect them.

Pink actually works so well with so many other colors: think of Pucci, Lilly Pulitzer, and the colors Jonathan Adler puts together. There is the salmony orange pink, the purply sky pink, the almost red pink, or the soft pink of seashells.

Of course, girls' and boys' rooms are not so different, although I've found girls do perhaps need more surfaces for their stuff. Pots for trinkets, trays for beauty products, and mirrors do not hurt. Girls also often need room for extra sleeping accommodations, since they usually have more sleepovers than boys. And girls usually need more space for their clothes; not just drawers, but ample hanging space. It's also important to have enough display space for favorite objects and collectibles, sometimes favorite dresses and shoes, soft toys lined up for a cuddle, and walls covered with drawings and paintings or little notes from best friends and aunts and uncles.

Children's rooms are places for self-discovery, spaces where they can create their own private worlds and get lost in their imaginations. The rooms in this chapter showcase a wide spectrum of styles, celebrating girl power in all its guises and showcasing the range of girls' creativity.

Eva's room is not pink–it's just the bedcover that makes it look that way. This shows the impact a bit of color can have on a room. How different would it look if the bed-spread were yellow, for example? I'm not sure she would be having as much fun!

Two girls share this room and each has her own bunk bed, ladder, closet, and desk area. Lots of shelves provide plenty of room for displaying their treasures, allowing them to personalize their spaces.

These two rooms, divided by a SLIDING DOOR, mirror each other. The clever use of space ensures each girl has PLENTY OF ROOM for sleeping, playing, and doing her homework, as well as good storage. The use of BOLD COLOR makes a strong and playful statement here.

The custom-made bunk is reminiscent of vintage furniture. It looks grown up, but its scale reminds us that it is for a child. The storage shelves on the left also serve as the ladder up to the top bunk.

A discarded archi-
tects model be-
comes a modern
dollhouse for a
selection of vintage
scaled-down furni-
ture, which comple-
ments the vintage
pieces in the room.

The built-in bed and storage look snazzy and keep this room well organized. The plush rug and plush ottomans add coziness and the Eames plywood elephant looks like he has just escaped from the bedcover.

In this home, each girl has a double bunk so she can invite friends over to stay. The loft sleeping quarters allow for cozy sitting and studying areas below. The butterfly stickers flutter around the room alighting on the wardrobes opposite the bunk.

Left: In a tall Victorian house, the youngest child has a simple room full of fun things. The bed, which is Scandinavian designed, extends as the child gets taller. The hanging chair looks like great fun.

Right: The foil leafy wallpaper is a great backdrop to the storage unit of books and soft toys. The white cuckoo clock appears to be floating on the wall.

Who says COWBOYS are only for boys? The vintage toys, primary colors, and the pink-and-white POLKA DOT nursery chair make this room very PLAYFUL AND PERFECT for the tomboy in the family.

A room with a view! In a Mies van der Rohe tower in Chicago, the floor-to-ceiling windows provide an ever-changing wallpaper, not just with the seasonal changes in the park outside, but with the enormous sky beyond. The patterned bedsheets and stuffed animals transform the bed into a cozy nest.

Left: The blue-sky wallpaper and the grass skirt and straw hat on the Eames coatrack take us back to our holidays and the warm days of summer. The patchwork crochet bedcover and embroidered pillow remind us where we really are.

Right: This little room is like a seaside cabin. The all-white interior is festooned with every color imaginable, in an array of patterns and stripes and pretty mobiles.

Jersey's room is a colorful place. Predominantly pink, the use of clashing orange and fuchsia prevents it from looking too Barbie-like. The contemporary artwork on the walls and the long, narrow worktable encourage her creativity.

Bold patterns every-
where. In a young
girl's room, the use
of a vintage wallpa-
per makes a unique
interior. The old fur-
niture painted white
gives it a new lease
on life, while the yel-
low chair brings a bit
of mid-century mod-
ern to the space. The
1950s toy pram is a
great prop.

PATTERNS AND DESIGNS

The giant hogweed mural on the wall makes the huge four-poster bed look small. This simple yet effective form of decoration is easy to create yourself using either paint and stencils or decals.

An off-the-shelf self-adhesive photo mural transforms this boy's room. Photo murals feature a wide array of scenes. The tree mural gives a calm feel to the space.

Whether it's a mural, cut-out decals, wallpaper, or paint, the walls are the one of the best and easiest places for pattern in a child's room. Of course, windows, bedcovers, pillows, and easy chairs are other great places to add pattern and require much less of a commitment.

We haven't been brave enough to do anything on the walls yet in our son's room. There is too much to choose from and we are just not sure where to do it and what method to use. But then, we are the same with our paintings in the rest of the house. We have several we love that are propped up here and there as we are not sure where to put them. And we actually quite like being able to move them around. So perhaps for us committing to wall art is simply too permanent. However, as our son's room is his, not ours, once he decides what he wants, we will be ready with paint, wallpaper, and scissors in hand!

Whenever I see a room that is decorated with a mural I am inspired; but I always think, if only I could do this, if only I could decide what to do. To that end, I have begun using non-permanent sticky-backed plastic (vinyl contact paper). In my shop last Christmas, I cut out different tree shapes from wood-effect plastic and stuck them on the walls. It took only about five minutes for each tree and the effect was unbelievable. Everyone loved it—we still have one on the wall, which we add to throughout the seasons, sticking on leaves in the spring, blossoms and then fruit in the summer, changing the leaves' colors in the fall, and then stripping it bare again in the winter when it gets decorated for the holidays! Our son loves it so much that every time he comes to the shop, more leaves and fruits are added, or removed, and we have fun starting all over again.

Using patterned fabrics is a simple and easy way to bring color and interest to a room. On the left, large-scale patterns work in a minimal interior, and on the right, small-scale patchwork textiles in different patterns and colors are used to their full extent.

Left: How simple and effective are black stripes on a white wall. The black could also be blackboard paint, which would allow the child to draw on the wall. The primary colors of the furniture and the rug add to the room's graphic pop.

Right: A large photo mural of penguins adds a humorous element to this boy's room: It looks like the penguins are dancing to the drumbeat.

An entire wall covered with a brightly COLORED MAP encourages the children to learn more about the WORLD, as well as being an exciting and FUN DESIGN FEATURE. This map includes people and ANIMALS that can be placed in their correct locations.

This type of non-permanent décor can easily be done in any room and the fact that it is always changing keeps any child forever interested in it. It's possible to find sticky-backed plastic in hundreds of colors and finishes, so the options are endless.

Today there are also so many wallpapers and fabrics designed with children in mind. I am continually buying rolls of wallpaper, but again have a hard time committing to hanging them. Fabrics, however, are a great resource, and are easier to decorate with on the fly, either as a throw over a bed or chair, as a wall hanging or sewn into throw pillows, adding just the right amount of pattern or color to a dull room. Using vintage fabrics is even better, as they are unique and therefore more personal. You can find themes and patterns to fit any genre or décor, whether it's the old Wild West, spaceships or boats, or exotic travel kitsch.

In this chapter, we have included a selection of decorating ideas, from wallpaper and sticky-backed plastic, to fabrics, mirrors, and simple but clever painting tricks. And as you will see, most of these ideas are simple enough to execute on your own. Really, when it comes to it, the inspiration is endless.

That is indeed the problem for us, too many ideas.

Comic-book favorites are used here in front of simple built-in bunks to create an exciting place to sleep. There is no end of characters you could use.

Using a simple selection of colors makes even the staircase up to bed more exciting. It can also help with organizing stuff, for example, putting shoes on the red stair.

79

A few simple SPACE-THEMED DECALS decorate the white wall in a boy's room. Decals are a quick and easy way to PERSONALIZE your child's room. Children can help or even DO IT THEMSELVES.

Wallpaper has come back into vogue. This house in Denmark is patterned from top to bottom making every room visually exciting for the young one's eyes. Mixing and matching color and pattern inspires our children to notice everything around them.

Josh's mom made these wall decorations for his room and found the amazing race-car bed. You can use either paint or decals to create a personalized room for your child. These wall designs can be added to or updated at any time. Your child can also enjoy helping!

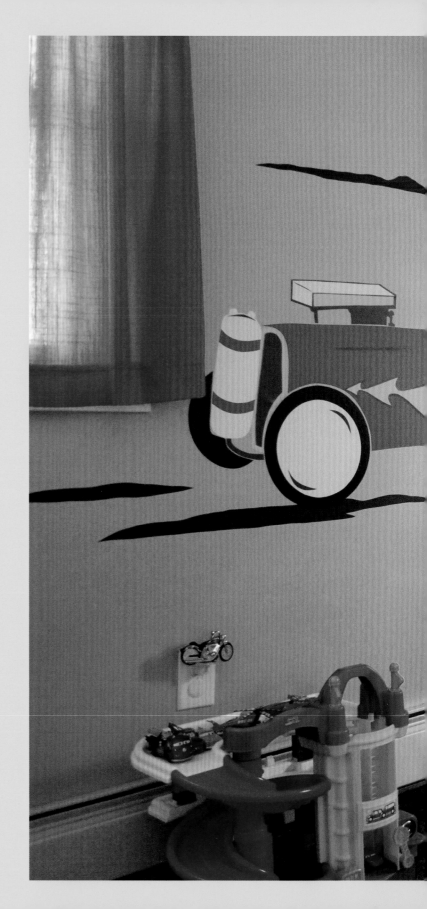

At home we used sticky-backed plastic cut into strips to make the tree trunk and branches. We added green leaf-shaped pieces and then orange circles to make it into an orange tree. You could make any kind of tree you like by adding blossoms, fruits, or autumn leaves. When it's bare you can decorate it with holiday baubles. This is something children can do easily and without too much mess!

Using the same fabric repeated on various items can make a complete interior scheme. In this young child's room, a colorful pattern has been used on the screen, the ottoman, and the pillows in the child's crib. Contrasting colors and patterned fabrics have been used elsewhere.

You cannot miss the alphabet in this room. The cupboard doors have been decorated with hand-painted letters to help inspire the child to learn.

Boys love pirates! In this room, the entire wall behind the bed is filled with a pirate-themed mural, with lots of characters and brightly colored birds. The pirate ship is bobbing up and down on the rough sea.

DISPLAY AND STORAGE

If you've got it, flaunt it. There is nothing better than being able to show off the stuff you love. Here, a collection of camels is on display for all to see. Encourage your child to collect something (even though it could become an obsession).

93

A raised bed allows for ample storage underneath for the toys and games. The sliding doors make it easy to access and quick to empty and fill. No excuse for an untidy room!

No matter how much storage we have in our home, it somehow never seems to be enough. If it's not the Legos, it's the board games. If it's not the paint and paper, it's the remote-control helicopter. But that is life with children! We have many cupboards and shelves devoted to the cause, but there can never be too many. We do try to be organized, but sometimes end up cramming so much into a cupboard that we dare not open it again, as the contents are sure to fall out all over the floor.

Of course, the downside to putting toys away (and especially overcrowding the available storage space) is that it's not always easy to find them again. "Dad, Dad, where is this? And where is that?" is what I hear several times a day when our son cannot remember where he has left his favorite car of the moment, or where his paints are.

Restricting children's toys to their rooms helps simplify this dilemma, although we prefer to keep the entire house playful and to come up with solutions throughout the home. Much of our storage is within the family space and not in our son's bedroom; this method means that the toys, games, and books in question can be easily put away at the end of the day, without too much problem in finding them again the next day. In the main living room, we have given away some of the George Nelson storage system to books and the Florence Knoll credenza now houses the Legos and board games. This way, we all know where everything is, making for a more harmonious environment.

In this London home lived in by a Scandinavian family, simple ideas rule. In the boys' room, the old sash window frames serve as great shelves for a small collection of model boats. While in the family room, the small selection of toys on display is always changing.

Old meets new in this room. An antique shop counter works well for storing all shapes and sizes. The plywood shelves are full of books and small toys, while the pierced plywood sheets hide the room's heating elements. There is plenty of storage in this room, but as always, perhaps not enough!

This space is shared by a mother and daughter. The stor-age-unit wall divides the room, providing privacy, while also storing supplies and toys. Messy items are housed in boxes.

Storage and display are linked, of course, because displaying items can be one way of storing them. We have lots of our own items we like on display throughout the house. We are avid collectors and we like to see our collections; they make up part of the décor of the room. Our vintage toys, games, and books are displayed in all our rooms and it makes us happy to be surrounded by them. I especially like to see our Lego projects out. In fact, I often find myself building something new every now and again, much to our son's dismay!

Getting the balance right and knowing what will work arranged out in the open and what to hide away is the hardest thing. Of course, collections, artwork, books, any beautiful or especially cherished objects, can work well displayed. Toys and games with many different pieces that can become unwieldy are best stored when they are not being used.

It can be difficult to get children to organize their toys and put them away; they tend to have many favorite things and they usually want to be able to see them. It's hard to shut your favorite stuffed bear away in the cupboard, or to put away pens in the drawer, when you know you will need them later. I too often find that whatever I do manage to squeeze into the cupboard is the item that causes questions later. "Where is my favorite fire engine?" for example, even though there are three others on the shelf.

In these pages you will find a selection of storage and display ideas and solutions, ranging from total order to total disarray. Depending on your décor and lifestyle, you will find your own balance of what will work for you.

In this house, wood- and cork-clad walls are the background for diverse storage and display areas. Built-in desks match the walls and provide ideal workspaces for growing children.

Left: This entrance hall extends the outdoors with its rustic furniture and tree-patterned wallpaper. Designed to be accessible, there are specific hooks, shelves, and boxes for each child, creating a well-organized and user-friendly space.

Below: A basic radiator acts as a good background for a boy's mementos.

Left: A wall of storage makes these objects and toys accessible for the family and ensures there are plenty of books for all to enjoy. The table's patterned frame and the colorful chairs make this a fun place to sit and read.

Right: Disc-shaped bulletin boards are a graphic way to group favorite photos and mementos. The Arad spiral shelf continues the circle theme and adds a fun design element while keeping the room well organized.

Lee Mindel says, "Children's rooms are an opportunity to inspire imagination and can be as sophisticated as their adult counterparts."

These shelves, built into an alcove, provide excellent display and storage. Less used items can live on the highest shelves, with more popular items lower down. The bottom shelf extends across the room, allowing favorite items to be in full view and easily accessible.

These open shelves provide an excellent way to SHOWCASE FAVORITE BOOKS, allowing their covers to be on display. And there is PLENTY OF ROOM to squeeze in more books!

KEEP CALM AND ROCK ON

In Dallas's room, the main design elements are storage and display. The green wall acts as a great backdrop to the art collection, and the blackboard area is a practical element that fits right in. The motto on the right says it all!

Every available surface in this room is covered with favorite things. Just wonder how many layers there are! Photos of family and friends line the ceiling, while rosettes of prizes won flank the wall. The entire space is an extension of the child's personality and life history. What can be wrong with that?

BEING OUTSIDE

There is nothing more fun than being outside, and up a tree, especially in your own tree house high above all the grown-ups. Here a simple A-frame structure fills the gap between the branches.

Architect Amir Sanei built this modern playhouse for his children. He used windows as doors for small people and to avoid it being too cutesy, topped it with galvanized corrugated steel.

Most of my happiest childhood memories are of being outside with my parents and my sister. Whether on the beach, in the countryside, or in town, I loved flying my kite, going fishing, digging deep in the sand, or rowing a boat on our local lake.

There is a great sense of freedom and discovery in playing outside, and simply being outdoors opens up an enormous array of activities for children. Whether it's as simple as kicking a ball into a makeshift goal or sleeping overnight in a tree house, there are so many different ways to have fun in the fresh air.

It's always fun to play house and kids love to build tents or forts, either indoors or out. It's where they can create their own special places, just for themselves and their friends, real and imaginary. Playhouses and teepees seem to be popular escape spaces for all children, giving them a space within their space to be whoever they want to be and to think about whatever they want; a place to go when feeling sad or just when they do want to be alone.

Many of the ideas in this chapter feature outdoor structures you can build yourself. There is nothing more fun than making one of these, out of fabric, blankets, or leftover building materials, custom-tailoring it for your needs and your space. Sometimes simply deciding what to build is the hardest part.

Even those of us without a weekend house or a backyard can find ways to spend time outside, whether it's at a park or a zoo, a city playground, or an occasional day trip away to the countryside or the beach. What's important is finding the spirit of adventure and playfulness that being outdoors can give us!

The back of the playhouse is clad in mirrors, allowing it to disappear somewhat into the garden. This little house was shortlisted for a R.I.B.A small-projects award and one client commissioned a full-sized house after seeing it.

Made from simple DIY-store materials, this capsule-shaped playhouse is wrapped with corrugated plastic and supported by a cross-bar frame to keep it steady. Inside, a rack system provides different levels capable of housing six kids for a sleepover!

Sometimes
there is NOTHING
BETTER than
to find a
PEACEFUL spot
all alone in
the GARDEN,
where you can
lose yourself.

A plain white teepee has been decorated with nature-themed stencils and its posts topped off with colorful yarn decorations. Teepees are enjoying great popularity these days and are easy to find—or, even better, you can make your own. These kids are playing with an array of craft materials, including yarn for wrapping and beads for threading all types of necklaces and decorations.

Another teepee, this one made from long sticks and draped with colorful crochet blankets that were sewn together to create a tent, makes an airy, light-filled escape for children. A perfect retreat from the midday sun.

Two boys having FUN! When the weather is fine, there is nothing better than BEING OUTSIDE, kicking a ball, swinging, or CLIMBING up into your TREE HOUSE.

This playhouse fills in a concrete strip next to the builder's house. This simple shed structure has become a great success. His kids love it and especially enjoy the full wall covered with blackboard paint, which creates an ever-changing backdrop in this well-used space.

Created using leftover materials from other outdoor projects, and based on the local pig shelters, this flying pigsty (also known as a Peter Pan house) is suspended between trees so that "pigs who cannot fly can land!" Their Dad completed this project over a couple of days off during the summer break.

Wish we were there on the sandy beach, with blue skies, body boards, and plenty of time to enjoy it all.

The Hope boys in their playroom area, busy building something new. The old chest is full of games. The bottom drawer acts as a booster to help them reach the top of the chest.

The staircase, from the entrance hall to the boys' top floor, is covered in "Frames" wall-paper, on which everyone can add or draw on his or her own portrait.

On the edge of London, this wider-than-average four-story townhouse is a child-friendly haven from the front door to the back. At the front of the house is the formal family room, where it seems that as soon as the boys enter, they calm down, sit properly, and are quiet and well behaved.

But as soon as they go through the double dividing doors into the playroom, everything changes! Every surface is covered with playful objects, whether they are new toys, vintage finds from the local thrift store, souvenirs from a recent holiday, or hand-me-downs from family or friends.

The playroom is central to the house and leads onto the kitchen/dining-room area. The space is open plan, yet clearly defined. In the playroom, the main feature is the Lego rug. This is a permanent feature and first-time guests or visitors often stumble over random wheels or action figures that blend in, perhaps too well, with the rug. The boys, ages four and seven, spend most days after school digging deep into this pile, giving them hours of pleasure.

In this home, the parents have an interest in everything playful, and this is reflected in the décor and in the children. Emmie, the mother, says, "Oscar Wilde once said 'All beautiful things belong to the same age.' I couldn't agree with him more! Our house is all about exactly that, mixing things up in terms of the style, the furniture, and the old together with the new; most importantly of all, it's about our children. Their presence permeates the house; not just their playroom."

The kitchen is where the boys stop, as soon as they get home, for their milk and cookies, before doing their homework or building their next Lego creation.

The family room/dining room is off the playroom area. The large table allows for drawing, studying, and great family mealtimes. The garden is beyond.

3 × 1 = 3	3 × 2 = 6
4 × 1 = 4	4 × 2 = 8
5 × 1 = 5	5 × 2 = 10
6 × 1 = 6	6 × 2 = 12
7 × 1 = 7	7 × 2 = 14
8 × 1 = 8	8 × 2 = 16
9 × 1 = 9	9 × 2 = 18
10 × 1 = 10	10 × 2 = 20

1 × 3 = 4	1 × 4 = 4
2 × 3 = 6	2 × 4 = 8
3 × 3 = 9	3 × 4 = 12
4 × 3 = 12	4 × 4 = 16
5 × 3 = 15	5 × 4 = 20
6 × 3 = 18	6 × 4 = 24
7 × 3 = 21	7 × 4 = 28
8 × 3 = 24	8 × 4 = 32
9 × 3 = 27	9 × 4 = 36
10 × 3 = 30	10 × 4 = 40

1 × 5 = 5	1 × 6 = 6
2 × 5 = 10	2 × 6 = 12
3 × 5 = 15	3 × 6 = 18
4 × 5 = 20	4 × 6 = 24
5 × 5 = 25	5 × 6 = 30
6 × 5 = 30	6 × 6 = 36
7 × 5 = 35	7 × 6 = 42
8 × 5 = 40	8 × 6 = 48
9 × 5 = 45	9 × 6 = 54
10 × 5 = 50	10 × 6 = 60

1 × 7 = 7	1 × 8 = 8
2 × 7 = 14	2 × 8 = 16
3 × 7 = 21	3 × 8 = 24
4 × 7 = 28	4 × 8 = 32
5 × 7 = 35	5 × 8 = 40
6 × 7 = 42	6 × 8 = 48
7 × 7 = 49	7 × 8 = 56
8 × 7 = 56	8 × 8 = 64
9 × 7 = 63	9 × 8 = 72
10 × 7 = 70	10 × 8 = 80

1 × 9 = 9	1 × 10 = 10
2 × 9 = 18	2 × 10 = 20
	3 × 10 = 30
	4 × 10 = 40
	× 10 = 50
	10 = 60
	10 = 70
	0 = 80

WILL LUKE

Left: Multiplication-table wallpaper adds a bit more fun to the play area. Look out for the deliberate error!

Right: The large Jonathan Adler fruit pillows provide comfy seating for quiet reading time in the family room.

The tree house at the end of the garden acts as a space for plenty of ball games. However, they do require adult participation!

In good weather, though, they are soon outside on the swing, in the tree house, or playing a quick game of football, with the dog, Max, often joining in.

Going upstairs, the first floor contains the grown-ups' rooms, but the staircase and landings are decked out with "Frames" wallpaper, which is quickly getting filled in by the boys and their friends. This wallpaper is a series of black frames on a white background that entices everyone passing by to draw a small picture. Every home should have it! Throughout the rooms and hallways are shelves of books, graphic objects, collections of semi-precious stones, and inspiring wall art, all very stimulating to the growing boys' minds.

The next floor houses the boys' rooms. Each has his own and it is quite obvious that they spend most of their time elsewhere in the house. These rooms are cozy and basic. The boys do spend time in them when friends come over for play dates, often making camps out of mattresses and quilts draped over chairs, and sometimes they take Legos up for a quiet moment, but mostly they use these rooms as getaway spaces. As these boys are so sociable and interactive, most of their time is spent in the playroom.

This house includes the boys from top to bottom. It allows them to feel comfortable wherever they are, yet the boys have their own spaces to retreat to whenever they need them. Emmie's top tip is: "I love to find things that will last the distance for kids. There are so many stages and phases they go through that you could spend your whole time redecorating in order to cater to the next stage of their lives. So I have steered away from child-sized furniture, themed wallpapers, etc. It's a waste of time and a financial drain!"

Legos, Legos every-where! The large braided rug is where lots of new creations are developed. Even the dog is trying to join in.

The boys have separate rooms. The younger one, room at left, has gathered plenty of his favorite things all around him. In the older boy's room, right, a race track on the wall and a cardboard Star Wars cutout protect the corner work area.

In the playroom area, the long work space is always ready to display new items. The bendy lights highlight the best of the selection. On the top shelf, portraits of English footballer Bobby Moore watch over the boys at play or at work.

ROLANDO HOUSE

Quiet time room, full of beautiful dolls and collectibles, pink poufs, and memories.

The house is full of a mix of pieces, from the past and the present, designer items with found objects. Here, contemporary photography provides a backdrop for a thrift-store deer.

In a duplex at the top of a high-rise building in London lives a nomadic family. They have traveled extensively, recently living in New York and, before that, Milan.

The mother, Florence, is a children's fashion and design specialist, consulting on brands and working on her blog, while the father works in an office. The family, with three children, live in great harmony in this quiet yet playful home. The style is urban, eclectic, quite minimal, yet also attached to quality and well-thought-out products. Florence says, "We like mixing up bits and pieces, past and present, designer items and things found in the street, from ethnic to pop. We have pieces we have gathered in flea markets in Italy, Belgium, France, the U.S., and the U.K. Things in this house are forever changing. New found objects and thrift-store finds appear and other items get put away. There are things hanging from the ceiling, and toys and objects on every surface."

There is no outdoor space attached to this home, and this suits the family just fine. "We are indoor people: we love spending time at home or in museums and galleries. The kids (and us parents) love to draw: we can all sit down with paper and crayons for hours, with good music in the background."

The kids love to play with their Legos, are especially into Star Wars figures at the moment, and also like watching films at home. The girls enjoy playing with their dolls and their vast collection of animals, which have been purchased at thrift stores near and far.

The living room displays eclectic pieces that have been gathered from flea markets in Italy, Belgium, France, the U.S., and the U.K. The collectibles and displays in this house are always changing.

The parents' collections of vintage toys, trains, and trucks are artfully displayed throughout the house.

The house has plenty of playful things in every room. Florence's mother has a large attic in her home where she has kept old toys handed down from generation to generation. "There is always something to find in the attic, like the yellow truck on my husband's bedside table," Florence says. "The old dolls in the girls' rooms are from mom's collection, as well as the little ski man and the folk creatures on the stairs." The line-up of tiny shoes that Florence used to wear as a child are also an attic find.

The many toys, trains, and trucks throughout the house are from the U.S., collected by the parents over the years. In addition, they have collections of fashion and photo magazines from the 1970s, 1980s, and 1990s, vinyl records, skateboards, cigar boxes, old keys, and tricycles from the 1930s to 1950s.

From the vintage toys passed down within the family, to the found objects collected from markets around the world, this is a household firmly rooted in the playful. Whether it's the artwork on the walls or the colors used throughout the home, every surface has something to catch the eye and to stimulate and inspire the brain. Florence loves to quote George Bernard Shaw, "We don't stop playing because we grow old, we grow old because we stop playing." As she says, "playing is universal, something everyone can understand. The playful home has a soul, it connects to emotions, to the child in all of us. Playing is a way of being together, and living in a playful home stimulates joy, putting us in a good mood: it's like taking vitamins."

The antique dolls and stuffed animals come from Florence's mother's huge attic, where she has kept generations of the family's old toys.

A variety of collections, from vintage trucks to statues and metal letters, are juxtaposed in open shelving.

A family of thrift-store deer share the mantelpiece.

Playing alone with one's **TOYS** is truly one of the greatest child-hood **JOYS**.

The girls share the room and often push their beds together. Their favorite dresses are ready, when there is a special occasion. The pompoms, made simply from net, soften the gray of the walls.

LIME HOUSE

Ready for fun, the hallway is hung with everything a boy needs for a quick getaway when "going out" is mentioned.

The central section of the George Nelson storage system has been given over to books and favorite toys and playthings. It seems the only way to keep some kind of order in the house!

A few years ago, when we moved from a small Victorian house into a large loft space, it took a while to get used to the open-plan layout and the new space it afforded. Not realizing at the time that we would be having a child move in several years later, we didn't think at all about making our home child friendly. So when we decided to adopt, we had to make certain modifications. We installed banisters on the open staircase, put re-strainers on the large metal windows, so they hardly opened, and juggled the bedrooms around.

Our son ended up having our bed-room with attached bathroom as his own; what's more, he now enjoys direct access to the small roof terrace, lucky boy. We hope he doesn't expect this for the rest of his life!

It was an easy task making the home feel playful and child friendly as we already had plenty of vintage toys, games, and objects actually made for children dotted around the place. We didn't, however, expect the entire house to be so taken over by his stuff.

Before he came home with us to live, we visited the home where he had been cared for to see his bedroom. It was small, but quite tidy and organized, with post-ers on the wall and his cars and remote-control toys in crates stacked up around the room. We saw that he was quite proud of what he had and liked to keep a lot of stuff on show, but also that he could put things away. Being a vintage furniture dealer, I always have a selection of items coming and going. Knowing that he liked orange and that we would also need lots of storage, I took advantage of this 1960s bedroom furniture. It fits well into the room and every drawer is crammed with stuff, whether it's toys or clothes.

Left: Legos adorn the Knoll credenza. Behind the grass-cloth doors are crates of bricks all in order of color and size. The John Pawson sofa is softened with pillows by Jonathan Adler.

Below: Gretel watches over all that goes on from her comfy bed.

Alien sketches hang on the bedroom wall, a joint effort by father and son. The sculpture is by Brian Willsher. The little star objects by Yoshimoto unfold and become cubes.

It took a little while to get some order back into our lives. The easiest way to adapt was to dedicate spaces throughout our home for his toys, books, and gadgets. This means that we can always get things put away, wherever they are left. Our furniture is vintage, from the mid-20th-century. Some is a little precious, but we believe it is made to be used. In the main living area, part of the George Nelson CSS storage system is given over to children's books, which are great to see displayed; it seems a shame to put them away as some of the covers are so colorful. In the den area the Florence Knoll grass-cloth-fronted credenza houses the board games, jigsaw puzzles, and Legos. In the dining area, where we all do some painting and drawing, the white cupboard doors are a great backdrop for an ever-changing wall of artwork.

We are lucky enough to have a spare bedroom, which has a platform bed. At the moment we have repurposed it as a "battle room." We found a suitcase full of scale models of World War II airplanes and tanks at the flea market and this inspired us to make a landscape model. We have hung airplanes on thread and added some bits of trees to make a landscape. Our son loves this area, and his friends are amazed by it.

From his bedroom there is a small enclosed roof terrace that leads onto the roof's communal area. Out here we have grown most of the plants from seed, watching them get bigger and flower. It's great to have this space as it gets us outside without having to go too far, and the communal area is a great running track for a very active boy.

Creating this playful home for our son after living a child-free existence for many years now has been challenging and rewarding.

We found a box of old airplane models that we are restoring. They will hang from the ceiling in the playroom.

On the Nelson shelves, art and bouncy balls mix well together.

Our son's room in the roof space is filled with vintage fabrics and rugs. We made the rocket from found stuff in the recycling bins where we live. The textile on the bed is "Robots" by Conran.

Left: The family of hands is impressed into the pin art sculpture blocks.

Right: On the roof terrace, decorated with Schultz furniture, the teepee gives some shade from the overhead sun. The remote-control cars are lined up for a race.

KURDAHL HOUSE

The building in which this apartment is located is clad in glass, so when dividing the internal loft space, glass walls were a natural choice. The children's rooms are right in the main living area, yet being behind glazed walls, they are their own enclosed spaces.

185

The open-plan layout allows one space to overlap with the next. On the wall between the kitchen space and a wall of artwork is a numeral block clock, helping the children to tell the time.

Squeezing a family with two children into what is supposed to be a one-bedroom apartment sounds challenging indeed. But it works in this glass-walled home as the space has been treated as a whole with the rooms open-plan–physically for the common areas and visually, at least, for the children's bedrooms.

The two children each have their own glazed-glass internal room. Their mother, Camilla, says, "It works really well. It is like one big room and when the kids play they are together with us all the time. The sound-proofing on the glass is better than with a normal wall, so it's good for when they sleep. If you have a cleaning issue this type of space is not for you, but we can live with finger-prints on the glass!"

The idea took a while to come together. "We knew when we bought the apartment that we would have to make two separate rooms for the kids. Since the building is all about glass, it was natural that we would make some rooms with glass." Initially the idea was for the two rooms to be side by side, but at the end they were built as two floors in order to keep the floor space and allow the main room to retain its spaciousness.

The children spend a lot of time in their rooms, especially in the lower-level space, as it is so connected to the rest of the home giving it the feeling that everyone is in the same room.

According to Camilla, the key to this playful home is that it is usable for the kids. "When the toys are put away, they are in places the kids can reach themselves. The colors must be fun and bright. We actually like white walls because the toys bring in plenty of color."

As a white box with glass walls, this space is like an adventure park for children, with the outside being as important as the inside. It has the open-plan advantages of a loft space, yet with distinct areas, each with its own use, and one in which the children are always included.

In the children's rooms, new and old mix together. Collections of favorite things are out on display, mounted on the wall, or arrayed on the shelves. The white walls throughout the apartment provide a canvas for the children's brightly colored toys and create a space that can constantly change.

A row of friendly ANIMALS from land and sea are LINED UP on the drop-front cabinet.

Color is an important part of the child-friendly home. Here it is found in the patchwork pillows and the Lego creations throughout the space.

RAINBOW HOUSE

The fifty-two-step spiral staircase is finished in a spectrum of colors, ending in a different hue at every floor level. It is wrapped in clear curved plastic, to be safe and to let the color shine through.

195

What better way to arrive for playtime than down a curvy slide, which links the top floor to this vast and colorful family room.

Hidden behind a classical flat-fronted Georgian facade is a house that is completely about having fun, a surprisingly playful zone for the whole family.

The Rainbow House, by Ab Rogers in collaboration with DA Studio, is designed to "move people through the space quickly with a blast of joy in the morning."

Upon entering, you come face to face with a spiral staircase of just over fifty steps. The staircase extends from the bottom to the top of the four-story house and looks as if it's wrapped in armored glass, interrupted only by the entry and exit for each floor. Ranging in tone from pastel to brights, the staircase is finished in some twenty-six colors, with each color range giving way to the hue for each given floor. At the top of the staircase are skylights that flood the area with light during the day.

The top floor contains the master bedroom with its revolving bed, circular bath, and wall of mirrors. The floor, designed by Richard Woods, is cartoon-like with red and white planks outlined in black. At one end of the room is a circular trapdoor opening onto a helter-skelter slide that drops you into the vast living and dining area below with its huge pop-up sitting, lounging, and playing area. The floor here is cartoon-like as well with large-scale flowers on a yellow background. The kitchen is at one end and a dining area consisting of a Saarinen table and chairs fills the mid-section.

The level below continues the playful theme with more patterned floors and fun elements, all of which create a magical escape from the reality just outside the front door. This home is a combination of large-scale design and pattern, simple yet incredibly fun elements, and a spectrum of cheerful color that fully embodies the spirit of playfulness.

The modular SITTING AREA can be arranged to make RAISED BEDS or sunken alcoves as the MOOD takes you.

The master bedroom, with its cartoon flooring and trapdoor to the level below–the playroom, where all the action is. In this home, playtime is for all, all the time!

MAKING STUFF

It's good to have plenty of materials on hand for the next craft project. In this home, they are artfully displayed to inspire creativity.

To make these God's Eyes, a craft project from kimmelkids.com, take 2 sticks, tie together to make a cross, and then wrap yarn around one stick onto the next as shown.

Making stuff and having fun often go together; but sometimes they don't! It can be frustrating when a project doesn't go according to plan. Thinking up new things to do and then figuring out how to do them can often be tricky.

I was raised with arts and crafts; when I was a child, my father was the instigator of all things creative. He worked in a candy factory and was often bringing home fancy wrappings and boxes and tins—we would spend hours cutting out and sticking and covering. Now with a son of my own we do endless craft projects. We have made life-size rockets, papier-mâché battle scenes for his model airplanes, and we spend a lot of time painting.

It's the journey from start to finish that makes crafts so satisfying; working with the various bits and pieces, putting them all together, and then at the end holding something that you have made, whatever it is, makes it all worthwhile. The same is true with cooking; we often prepare dinner together, one of us peeling the vegetables, one of us chopping, and one of us watching the timer. We have made what seems like every cookie recipe we have come across.

Interacting with kids in this way puts us all on the same level: we can be silly with simple paper masks made out of paper bags, or we can make folded paper toys into games that seem to last forever; in short, we can be kids again ourselves. It's amazing how many memories come floating back once you get the tissue paper and glue out.

It is a great feeling, getting dirty and covered in stuff. It's great to laugh out loud and, of course, it is even more great to applaud and praise your kids for their ability and creativity.

Hunting high and low for new things to do at home, we have found many great projects on various Web sites. This chapter is a selection of some that we have loved doing together.

Left: There is nothing that makes a child more proud than to see his or her work framed and hanging on the wall. Here are two family portraits, or is the one on the left a princess?

Right: Our family dining area becomes an art studio when required. While we all love our vintage pieces, with kids around you cannot be too precious with your furniture!

A PAPER DOLL HOUSE
from madebyjoel.com

This is a FUN and EASY way to make simple paper houses with minimal and MODERN folded furniture. Using pages from magazines creates great color schemes and VISUAL EFFECTS. You can use the template Joel provides on his Web site.

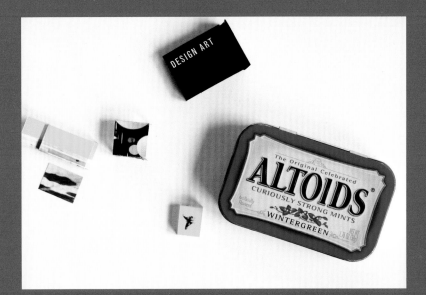

209

TOTEM POLES
by khali

Your children will have a MAGICAL TIME playing make BELIEVE with these totem poles crafted from POSTAGE TUBES.

You'll need:
Postage tubes in various sizes
Masking tape
Paint
Paintbrush
Colored cardstock
Colored pens or pencils
Glue

1. Decide on the number of colors you wish to have along the length of your postage tubes. Place strips of masking tape around the width of your postage tubes to mark the borders of each color.
2. Paint the sections of your postage tubes in different colors and allow to dry.
3. Use colored pens and pencils to draw designs (such as faces) on colored cardstock for the front of your totem pole.
4. Cut out your designs and attach to the front of the paper tubes with glue. Then act out imaginary stories using them!

POETRY RIVER

A great project from madebyjoel.com
Cut out a winding river shape in blue paper. Write some favorite words, activities, and memories on some pebble-shaped cutouts and arrange the words along the river to make up phrases. Add some natural materials, such as pebbles and twigs.

CARDBOARD ROBOTS

A great project from madebyjoel.com
Cut out various robot body-part shapes in cardboard, then paint and decorate them as you wish. Use velcro to attach the pieces together to make a robot family. Add cardboard feet, inserted into the body as shown.

Rubber floors, laminated tabletops, and plastic chairs are perfect, practical elements for areas like this one, where we let our children's creativity have free rein. Here, all the surfaces are scrubbable.

BOX AQUARIUM
from madebyjoel.com

Cut a box into a frame shape as shown, leaving the top and bottom intact and with extra flaps on both to attach the box to a wall. Cut full-length slits along the top. Use the extra cardboard to cut out and paint FISH, CRAB, and SNAIL SHAPES. Tie threads around them and then pull the threads up through the slits and tie each to a button. Sliding the buttons along the slits gives the beautiful effect of SEA CREATURES swimming around the aquarium.

Simple Flowerpots by kimmelkids.com Paint small terra-cotta flowerpots in various bright colors and then stencil with a daisy motif. You can also use other stencil designs or create patterns using contact paper. The possibilities are endless.

FELT FLOWERS
by khali

Whether you're feeling the WARM RAYS of spring or settling into autumn, this felt flower bouquet is bound to BRIGHTEN YOUR DAY.

3 felt sheets (we used green, yellow, and fuchsia)
6 green pipe cleaners
scissors

1. Cut six circles approximately 4 inches in diameter from the fuchsia felt sheet and six circles approximately 1½ inches in diameter from the yellow felt sheet.
2. Make a small cut in the center of each felt circle.
3. Tie a knot in the end of each pipe cleaner. Thread a yellow and fuchsia circle onto the pipe cleaner and push down to the knot at the other end.
4. Cut six lengths of green felt and tie around the pipe cleaner stem.

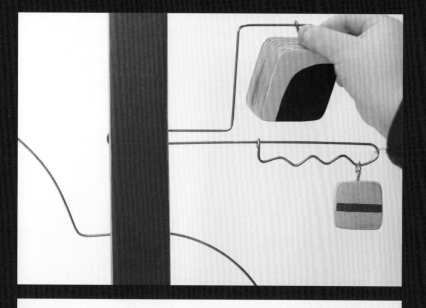

MODERN TREE MOBILE

from madebyjoel.com

Attach a couple different lengths of PAINTED WOOD to a larger slab base. Drill a few holes along the sides of the uprights, into which you will insert VARIOUS WIRE SHAPES, as shown. From these you can hang painted wooden blocks of DIFFERENT SHAPES and sizes painted with a design of your choice.

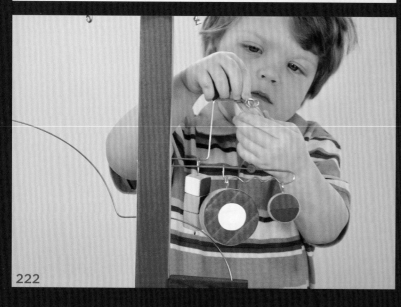

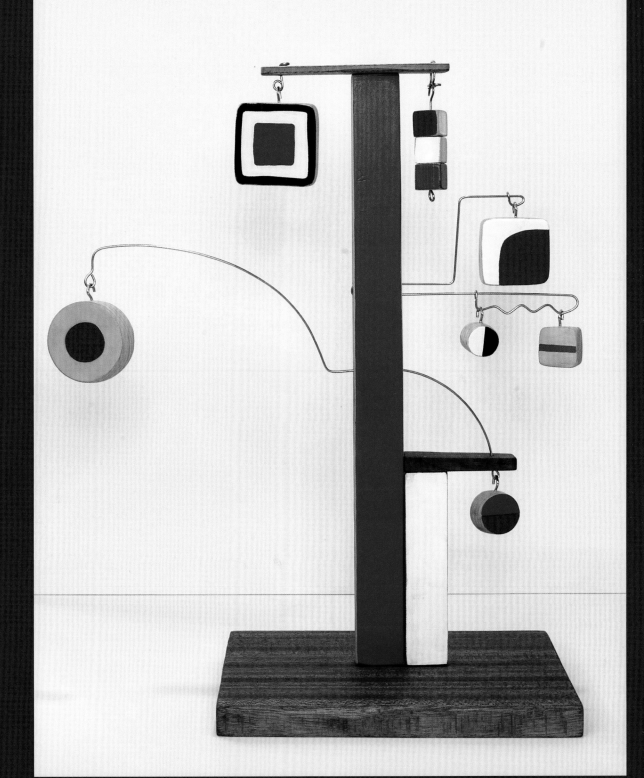

Felt pictures by kim-melkids.com. Boards wrapped in felt serve as backgrounds for ever-changing picture creations made from felt scraps. You can cut out different shapes in a variety of colors to create the pictures you want.

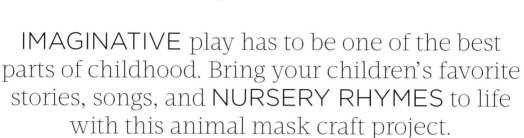

ANIMAL MASK
by khali

IMAGINATIVE play has to be one of the best parts of childhood. Bring your children's favorite stories, songs, and NURSERY RHYMES to life with this animal mask craft project.

You'll need:
2 pieces of cardstock
Pink and gray colored paper
Glue
Pencil
Scissors
Hole punch
Scotch tape
2 pieces of ribbon

1. Draw an outline of a rabbit mask onto a piece of cardstock or download the templates.
2. Cut out the mask.
3. Draw the inside of the rabbit ears on pink colored paper, cut out, and glue to the mask.
4. Punch holes in either side of the mask.
5. Thread ribbon through each hole and tie a knot to secure.

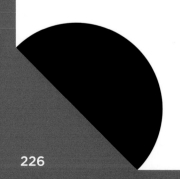

Left: Make a teepee. Take a few long sticks and tie them together at the top. Drape with some simple fabric, such as a bedsheet, a blanket, or an old curtain. Presto! You instantly have a playhouse for the little one.

Right: Eames houses of cards are a time-less toy for all to enjoy. Here the giant ones are even more fun.

Tin Can Walkie Talkies from madebyjoel.com. Take a couple of clean cans and use a hammer and nail to make a small hole on the base of each. Push the one end of a length of string into each can and tie in a secure knot. Pull hard between two kids, then talk and listen. It's fun to decorate the cans with colored stickers.

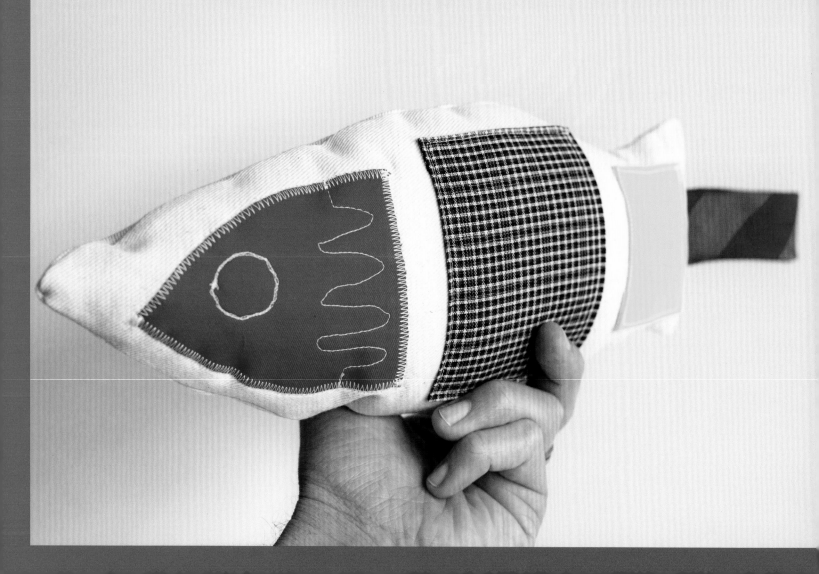

FISH PILLOW

from madebyjoel.com

Cut out two **FISH SHAPES** in a natural-colored fabric, at whatever size you want. Find some smaller scraps for color accents and the tail. Sew the colored squares and accents onto the fish shape. Put the two fish shapes together, decorated sides face to face. **STITCH** around the outer edge leaving the tail section open. Turn right-side out and stuff full of cotton or old cloth. Insert a **TAIL-SHAPED** piece of fabric, perhaps a bit of an old tie, into the open end and stitch up to close the fish.

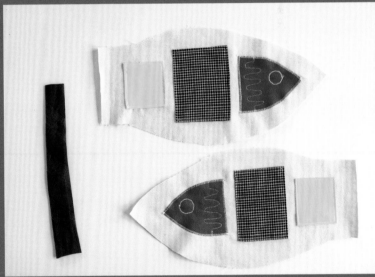

233

FLORENTINES
by Splat Cooking

YIELD: APPROXIMATELY 24 COOKIES

5¼ tablespoons butter
5 tablespoons superfine sugar
3 tablespoons all-purpose flour
2 ounces chopped hazelnuts
2 ounces chopped mixed peel (candied citrus peel)
1 ounce golden raisins, chopped
1 ounce candied cherries, washed and chopped
2¾ ounces dark chocolate
2¾ ounces milk chocolate
¼ teaspoon freshly ground whole allspice

You will need: Baking sheet, parchment paper or silicone baking sheet, measuring spoons, saucepan, wooden spoon, timer, oven mitts, microwave-safe bowl

How to make Florentines: Wash your hands!

1. Ask an adult to preheat the oven to 350 degrees F. Grease a baking sheet and line it with parchment paper or a silicone baking sheet. (Greasing the baking sheet first helps the parchment paper stick and keeps it from sliding around.)

2. Ask an adult to watch while you melt the butter and sugar together in a saucepan. Remove from the heat and add the flour, hazelnuts, candied peel, golden raisins, and candied cherries. Mix thoroughly.

3. Place teaspoonfuls of the batter on the baking sheet. Leave plenty of space around each because the batter will spread.

4. Ask an adult to put them in the oven to bake for about 10 minutes until golden. Remove from the oven and neaten the edges before they harden.

5. Place the dark and milk chocolates in a microwave-safe bowl. Heat on medium for 1 minute, then continue in 10 second bursts until the chocolate is almost melted. Stir to melt the last bits. Add the allspice.

6. Spread the chocolate over the flat side of the cookies. Chill in the refrigerator to set the chocolate.

MINI CRUMBLE
by Splat Cooking

YIELD: 6 MINI CRUMBLES OR 1 LARGE CRUMBLE

6 apples
A mix of pears, plums, and peaches (6 in total)
6¼ tablespoons superfine sugar
1 teaspoon ground cinnamon
For the crumble topping:
1½ cups all-purpose flour
7 tablespoons butter, chilled and diced
½ cup packed light brown sugar

You will need: Peeler, paring knife, round-bladed knives for children, mixing bowls, spoons, 6 ramekins or a pie dish, baking sheets, timer, oven mitts

How to make Fruit Crumbles: Wash your hands!

1. Ask an adult to preheat the oven to 350 degrees F and to help you peel and core the apples and pears, and to peel and pit the plums and peaches. Using a round-bladed knife, cut into quarters and then cut the quarters into small pieces.
2. In a medium bowl, mix together the fruit, sugar, and cinnamon. Divide the mixture among the ramekins or place into one pie dish. Spoon over any juice.
3. To make the crumble topping, put the flour and butter in a medium bowl and rub together with your fingertips until the mixture looks like fine breadcrumbs. Stir in the brown sugar.
4. Spoon the topping over the fruit and press down very gently with the back of the spoon. Place the ramekins or pie dish onto a baking sheet and and ask an adult to place in the oven. Bake until golden and bubbling, about 20 to 30 minutes.

Designer Credits

Photography Credits

Acknowledgments

Thanks to all who helped make this book happen, they know who they are!!
Everyone has been so enthusiastic, and while we have tried to include as many homes as we could, it has been impossible to use every image we collected.
It has been great working on a book that is about living and about making your home work for the entire family when children arrive in your life.
A special thanks to my partner and to our son, who inspired me to write this book.
Thanks to all at Rizzoli, especially to Ellen Nidy and Aoife Wasser for their patience and understanding with my new family life.